Ireland

Everything You Need to Know

Introduction to Ireland

Welcome to the captivating world of Ireland, the Emerald Isle that has long enchanted travelers with its stunning landscapes, rich history, and vibrant culture. Situated in the North Atlantic, Ireland is an island nation known for its lush green countryside, dramatic coastlines, and ancient monuments. From bustling cities to quaint villages, each corner of this enchanting land offers a unique glimpse into its storied past and dynamic present.

Steeped in mythology and folklore, Ireland boasts a heritage that stretches back thousands of years. The island's ancient Celtic roots are evident in its numerous megalithic sites, such as Newgrange and the Hill of Tara, which predate the Egyptian pyramids. Over the centuries, Ireland has been shaped by waves of invaders and settlers, from the Vikings to the Normans, each leaving their mark on the land and its people.

The history of Ireland is marked by struggle and resilience, from the early Christian monks who preserved learning during the Dark Ages to the centuries-long struggle for independence from British rule. The Irish War of Independence and the subsequent partition of the island led to decades of conflict known as the Troubles, which finally gave way to the peace process and the Good Friday Agreement in 1998.

Today, Ireland is a vibrant modern nation, known for its warm hospitality, lively music and dance, and literary legacy. Dublin, the capital city, is a bustling metropolis with a rich cultural scene, including the world-famous Trinity College and the historic Book of Kells. Other cities, such as Belfast, Galway, Cork, and Limerick, each offer their own unique charm and attractions, from historic landmarks to lively pubs and restaurants.

But Ireland is more than just its cities. The countryside is dotted with picturesque villages, rolling hills, and serene lakes, making it a paradise for outdoor enthusiasts and nature lovers. Along the rugged coastline, visitors can marvel at the dramatic cliffs of Moher, explore the otherworldly landscapes of the Giant's Causeway, or take a scenic drive along the Wild Atlantic Way.

Irish culture is celebrated around the world for its music, literature, and folklore. Traditional Irish music and dance are an integral part of daily life, with lively sessions held in pubs and cultural centers throughout the country. Ireland's rich literary tradition includes such luminaries as James Joyce, W.B. Yeats, and Seamus Heaney, whose works continue to inspire readers around the globe.

In this book, we will take you on a journey through the fascinating history, culture, and landscapes of Ireland, exploring its ancient heritage, modern society, and everything in between. Whether you're planning a trip to the Emerald Isle or simply want to learn more about this enchanting land, join us as we uncover the wonders of Ireland, from its misty moors to its bustling cities, and everything in between. Welcome to Ireland – céad míle fáilte!

The History of Ireland: From Ancient Myth to Modern Nation

In delving into the history of Ireland, one must first navigate through the mists of ancient mythology that shroud its origins. According to legend, the island was populated by a race known as the Tuatha Dé Danann, who were said to possess magical powers and divine ancestry. Tales of heroes like Cú Chulainn and Finn McCool further weave the tapestry of Ireland's mythical past, blending folklore with history in a captivating narrative that continues to inspire and intrigue.

Moving beyond the realm of myth, archaeological evidence reveals a more concrete understanding of Ireland's early inhabitants. The island's megalithic sites, such as Newgrange and the Hill of Tara, date back thousands of years, pre-dating even the Egyptian pyramids. These ancient structures bear witness to the ingenuity and craftsmanship of Ireland's earliest settlers, who left behind a legacy that still mystifies archaeologists and historians today.

As the centuries passed, Ireland became a focal point of Celtic culture and civilization. The arrival of the Celts around 500 BCE marked a significant turning point in the island's history, introducing new languages, customs, and beliefs that would shape its identity for centuries to come. The Celtic influence is evident in Ireland's language, art, and mythology, as well as its unique system of governance, which was characterized by tribal kingships and a complex social hierarchy.

The spread of Christianity in the early Middle Ages brought about profound changes in Irish society. Missionaries like St. Patrick and St. Columba played instrumental roles in converting the pagan population to Christianity, establishing monastic settlements that became centers of learning and culture. The illuminated manuscripts produced by Irish monks, such as the Book of Kells, are testament to the artistic and intellectual achievements of this golden age of Irish Christianity.

However, Ireland's newfound faith did not shield it from external threats. In the 9th century, the island was targeted by Viking raids, leading to centuries of conflict and instability. The Vikings established settlements along the coast, such as Dublin and Waterford, which would eventually grow into thriving urban centers. The arrival of the Normans in the 12th century further reshaped Ireland's political landscape, introducing feudalism and feudal institutions that would leave a lasting impact on Irish society.

The 16th and 17th centuries saw Ireland thrust into the midst of the Tudor conquest and the subsequent plantation of Ulster, which sought to establish English control over the island and suppress Irish Catholicism. The brutal repression of Irish culture and religion, coupled with the confiscation of land and resources, sparked centuries of resistance and rebellion, culminating in the Irish War of Independence and the establishment of the Irish Free State in 1922.

Yet, even in the face of adversity, Ireland persevered, emerging as a proud and independent nation with a rich cultural heritage and a vibrant modern society. Today, Ireland stands as a testament to the resilience and determination of its people, who have weathered the storms of history to forge a bright and promising future. From ancient myth to modern nation, the story of Ireland is a testament to the enduring spirit of its people and the enduring legacy of its past.

Celtic Roots: Exploring Ireland's Ancient Heritage

To truly understand Ireland's essence, one must delve deep into its Celtic roots, for they form the very foundation upon which the nation's identity is built. The Celts, an Indo-European people, began migrating to Ireland around 500 BCE, bringing with them a rich tapestry of language, art, and tradition that would shape the island's culture for millennia.

The Celtic society was organized into tribes, each governed by a king or chieftain and bound together by a shared language and religion. They were skilled artisans, renowned for their intricate metalwork, elaborate jewelry, and intricate knotwork designs that adorned everything from weapons to everyday objects. The intricate patterns of Celtic art, with their interwoven motifs and symbolic imagery, continue to captivate and inspire artists and craftsmen to this day.

At the heart of Celtic society lay a deep reverence for nature and the natural world. The Celts believed in the existence of sacred places, such as holy wells, sacred groves, and burial mounds, where they conducted rituals and ceremonies to honor the gods and spirits of the land. The ancient Celtic calendar was based on the cycles of the sun and moon, with seasonal festivals marking the changing of the seasons and the agricultural calendar.

Central to Celtic spirituality was the belief in the interconnectedness of all living things, a concept reflected in their mythology and folklore. The Celtic pantheon was populated by a diverse array of gods and goddesses, each associated with different aspects of nature and human experience. Deities like Lugh, the god of light and craftsmanship, and Brigid, the goddess of hearth and home, were revered as protectors and patrons of the people.

One of the most enduring symbols of Celtic spirituality is the concept of the Otherworld, a mystical realm that exists beyond the physical world. In Celtic mythology, the Otherworld is a place of eternal youth and beauty, inhabited by supernatural beings such as fairies, elves, and spirits. It is a realm of magic and mystery, where the boundaries between the mortal and divine are blurred, and anything is possible.

The arrival of Christianity in Ireland in the early Middle Ages brought about profound changes in Celtic society. Missionaries like St. Patrick and St. Columba sought to Christianize the pagan population, incorporating elements of Celtic spirituality into their teachings and rituals. The result was a unique fusion of Christian and Celtic beliefs, evident in the many saints and holy sites that dot the Irish landscape.

Despite the passage of time and the influence of external forces, Ireland's Celtic heritage remains a source of pride and inspiration for its people. From the intricate designs of Celtic art to the timeless tales of Celtic mythology, the legacy of the Celts continues to shape and enrich Ireland's cultural landscape. In exploring Ireland's ancient heritage, we uncover not just the story of a people, but the soul of a nation.

Viking Invasions and Norman Conquests: Shaping Ireland's Destiny

The Viking invasions and Norman conquests represent pivotal chapters in Ireland's tumultuous history, shaping its destiny in profound and lasting ways. The Vikings, fierce warriors and skilled seafarers from Scandinavia, first raided Ireland's shores in the late 8th century, sowing chaos and fear among the native population. Their longships, with their dragon-headed prows, struck terror into the hearts of coastal communities, as they plundered monasteries, sacked settlements, and seized land for themselves.

Yet, the Vikings were not mere marauders; they were also traders and settlers who established lasting settlements along the coast. Cities like Dublin, Waterford, Wexford, and Limerick were founded by the Vikings, who transformed them into bustling centers of trade and commerce. They introduced new technologies, such as shipbuilding and coinage, and left an indelible mark on Irish society and culture.

The Viking Age in Ireland reached its zenith in the 9th and 10th centuries, as the Norsemen expanded their influence and power throughout the island. They established alliances with local chieftains, intermarried with Irish families, and adopted elements of Gaelic culture and language. By the 11th century, the Vikings had become fully integrated into Irish society, their legacy evident in the urban landscapes and cultural institutions they helped to create.

But the Viking era was soon overshadowed by the arrival of the Normans in the 12th century, who would leave an even greater impact on Ireland's history. Led by the formidable figure of Strongbow, the Normans invaded Ireland at the invitation of the exiled King of Leinster, Dermot MacMurrough, who sought their assistance in reclaiming his throne. In 1169, Strongbow and his knights landed in Ireland, sparking a chain of events that would forever alter the course of Irish history.

The Norman conquest of Ireland was characterized by brutal warfare, as the invaders sought to subdue the native Irish and impose their authority over the island. They built imposing castles and fortifications, such as Trim Castle and Dublin Castle, to consolidate their power and control. They introduced feudalism and feudal institutions, establishing a system of land tenure that favored their own nobility and marginalized the Gaelic chieftains.

Despite their military prowess, the Normans encountered fierce resistance from the native Irish, who fought valiantly to preserve their independence and cultural identity. The struggles of figures like Brian Boru and Hugh O'Neill became the stuff of legend, as they waged guerrilla warfare against the invaders and rallied their people to defend their homeland. Yet, in the end, the Normans prevailed, establishing English rule over Ireland and laying the groundwork for centuries of conflict and division.

The legacy of the Viking invasions and Norman conquests continues to reverberate through Ireland's history, politics, and society to this day. The scars of conquest run deep, shaping the relationships between Ireland and its neighbors, and fueling centuries of resistance and rebellion. Yet, amidst the tumult and turmoil, the spirit of the Irish endures, a testament to the resilience and determination of a people who have faced adversity with courage and defiance.

The Irish War of Independence: A Nation's Struggle for Freedom

The Irish War of Independence stands as a defining moment in Ireland's quest for self-determination and freedom from British rule. It was a period of intense conflict and upheaval that spanned from 1919 to 1921, marking the culmination of centuries of resistance to English domination. The seeds of rebellion had been sown long before, with the failed uprisings of 1798, 1848, and 1867, but it was not until the aftermath of World War I that the Irish people rose up en masse to demand their independence.

The war was waged primarily by the Irish Republican Army (IRA), a guerrilla force comprised of volunteers from across Ireland, who carried out a campaign of ambushes, assassinations, and sabotage against British forces and institutions. Their tactics were bold and audacious, targeting police barracks, military convoys, and government installations with precision and determination. The IRA's leader, Michael Collins, emerged as a charismatic and enigmatic figure, orchestrating the guerrilla campaign from the shadows while negotiating with British authorities behind the scenes.

The British response to the IRA's insurgency was swift and brutal, with reprisals and atrocities committed on both sides. The infamous Black and

Tans, a paramilitary force recruited from ex-servicemen, were deployed to Ireland to quell the rebellion, but their heavy-handed tactics only served to inflame tensions and escalate the violence. The conflict descended into a cycle of reprisals and counter-reprisals, with civilians caught in the crossfire and atrocities committed on both sides.

The turning point of the war came with the signing of the Anglo-Irish Treaty in December 1921, which established the Irish Free State as a self-governing dominion within the British Commonwealth. While hailed as a victory by some, the treaty was deeply divisive within Ireland, leading to a bitter civil war between those who accepted it and those who rejected it. The country was plunged into a fratricidal conflict that pitted former comrades-in-arms against each other, tearing families and communities apart in the process.

In the end, the pro-treaty forces emerged victorious, securing control of the fledgling Irish state and establishing the foundations of modern Ireland. Yet, the scars of the civil war would linger for generations, dividing Irish society and shaping its politics and identity in the years to come. The Irish War of Independence was a tumultuous chapter in Ireland's history, but it was also a testament to the courage and resilience of a people who refused to be cowed by oppression and injustice.

The Troubles: Ireland's Journey to Peace

The Troubles represent one of the darkest chapters in Ireland's recent history, a period of protracted conflict and sectarian violence that engulfed Northern Ireland for over three decades. Beginning in the late 1960s and lasting until the late 1990s, the Troubles were fueled by deep-seated divisions between the predominantly Catholic nationalist community, who sought reunification with the Republic of Ireland, and the predominantly Protestant unionist community, who wished to remain part of the United Kingdom.

The roots of the Troubles can be traced back to the partition of Ireland in 1921, which created the separate entities of Northern Ireland and the Irish Free State. The Catholic nationalist minority in Northern Ireland faced discrimination and marginalization at the hands of the Protestant-dominated government, leading to widespread grievances and resentment. Civil rights protests in the late 1960s, inspired by the broader civil rights movement in the United States, were met with violence and repression, sparking the onset of the Troubles.

The conflict quickly escalated into a cycle of violence, with paramilitary groups on both sides carrying out bombings, shootings, and assassinations in pursuit of their respective goals. The Provisional Irish Republican Army (IRA), a paramilitary organization dedicated to the reunification of Ireland through armed struggle, waged a campaign of guerrilla warfare against British security forces and unionist paramilitaries. Meanwhile, loyalist paramilitary groups, such as the Ulster Volunteer Force (UVF) and the Ulster Defence Association (UDA), targeted Catholics and republicans in a campaign of terror and intimidation.

The Troubles exacted a heavy toll on the people of Northern Ireland, with thousands killed or injured and countless more traumatized by the violence. The conflict spilled over into the Republic of Ireland and mainland Britain, as bombings and assassinations carried out by paramilitary groups struck fear and uncertainty into the hearts of civilians. The British government's response to the Troubles, including the deployment of troops and the implementation of emergency laws, only served to exacerbate tensions and deepen divisions within society.

Despite the seemingly intractable nature of the conflict, efforts to find a peaceful resolution continued throughout the Troubles. Diplomatic initiatives, such as the Sunningdale Agreement in 1973 and the Anglo-Irish Agreement in 1985, sought to address the underlying causes of the conflict and pave the way for reconciliation. However, it was not until the late 1990s that a breakthrough was achieved, with the signing of the Good Friday Agreement in 1998.

The Good Friday Agreement, also known as the Belfast Agreement, represented a historic compromise between the conflicting parties, laying the groundwork for power-sharing government in Northern Ireland and establishing mechanisms for addressing issues of justice, human rights, and decommissioning of weapons. While the peace process has faced numerous challenges and setbacks in the years since, Northern Ireland has largely enjoyed a period of relative peace and stability, allowing its people to move forward and build a more hopeful future.

Ireland Today: A Vibrant Modern Society

Today, Ireland stands as a vibrant modern society, a far cry from the troubled times of its past. From bustling cities to picturesque countryside, the Emerald Isle is a tapestry of diversity and dynamism, where tradition meets innovation in a harmonious blend. At the heart of Ireland's modern identity is its people, who are renowned for their warmth, wit, and resilience in the face of adversity.

Dublin, the capital city, is a bustling metropolis that pulsates with energy and creativity. Its streets are lined with historic landmarks, trendy boutiques, and lively pubs, where locals and visitors alike gather to share stories and laughter over a pint of Guinness. The city's cultural scene is thriving, with world-class museums, galleries, and theaters showcasing the best of Irish art, literature, and music.

Beyond Dublin, Ireland is a patchwork of vibrant communities and picturesque landscapes. In the west, the rugged coastline of the Wild Atlantic Way beckons adventurers and nature lovers alike, with its dramatic cliffs, pristine beaches, and charming seaside villages. In the south, the rolling hills of the countryside are dotted with quaint towns and villages, where time seems to stand still amid the tranquility of rural life.

Irish society is characterized by its strong sense of community and solidarity, with neighbors looking out for one another and coming together in times of need. Volunteerism and philanthropy are deeply ingrained in the national psyche, with countless organizations and charities dedicated to supporting those less fortunate. The spirit of generosity and compassion is evident in the countless acts of kindness and solidarity that occur daily across the country.

In recent years, Ireland has emerged as a global leader in technology and innovation, with companies like Google, Facebook, and Apple establishing European headquarters in Dublin. The thriving tech sector has fueled economic growth and job creation, attracting talent from around the world and positioning Ireland as a hub of creativity and entrepreneurship.

Yet, amidst the rapid pace of change and development, Ireland remains deeply rooted in its traditions and heritage. The Gaelic language, though not widely spoken, is experiencing a revival, with efforts underway to promote its use and preservation. Traditional music and dance continue to flourish, with festivals and sessions held throughout the year to celebrate Ireland's rich cultural heritage.

In politics, Ireland has undergone significant transformation in recent years, with the repeal of restrictive laws on abortion and same-sex marriage signaling a shift towards a more progressive and inclusive society. Women and minorities are increasingly represented in positions of leadership and influence, reflecting the country's commitment to equality and social justice.

As Ireland looks to the future, it faces challenges and opportunities alike. Climate change, economic inequality, and social division are among the pressing issues that demand attention and action. Yet, the spirit of resilience and determination that has defined Ireland throughout its history continues to burn bright, guiding the country forward into a brighter and more hopeful tomorrow.

Geography and Climate: The Varied Landscapes of Ireland

Ireland's geography is as diverse as it is stunning, encompassing a range of landscapes that showcase the island's natural beauty and richness. From rugged coastlines to rolling green hills, each region offers its own unique blend of scenery and charm. The island is situated in the North Atlantic Ocean, off the western coast of Europe, and is divided into two main political entities: the Republic of Ireland in the south and Northern Ireland in the north.

One of Ireland's most striking features is its coastline, which stretches for over 3,000 miles and boasts some of the most dramatic cliffs and rock formations in the world. The Cliffs of Moher, located on the west coast, rise to heights of over 700 feet above the Atlantic Ocean, offering breathtaking views of the surrounding seascape. Further north, the Giant's Causeway is a UNESCO World Heritage Site renowned for its hexagonal basalt columns, formed by volcanic activity millions of years ago.

Inland, Ireland's landscape is characterized by rolling green hills and lush countryside, earning it the nickname "the Emerald Isle." The central plains of the country are dotted with quaint villages, historic towns, and picturesque farmland, where sheep graze peacefully against a backdrop of verdant pastures. The River Shannon, Ireland's longest river, meanders through the heart of the country, providing both a vital waterway and a scenic route for travelers.

To the west, the Connemara region is a rugged wilderness of mountains, lakes, and bogs, where Gaelic culture and tradition thrive amidst the untamed beauty of the landscape. The Burren, located in County Clare, is a unique karst limestone plateau characterized by its barren and lunar-like appearance, dotted with ancient ruins and rare flora. Meanwhile, in the southeast, the Wicklow Mountains offer a haven for hikers and outdoor enthusiasts, with their craggy peaks and hidden valleys.

Ireland's climate is influenced by its proximity to the Atlantic Ocean, resulting in mild temperatures and abundant rainfall throughout the year. The west coast tends to be wetter and windier than the east, with the highest levels of precipitation occurring in the mountains and coastal regions. Summers are generally cool and damp, while winters are mild with occasional frost and snow in the higher elevations.

Overall, Ireland's geography and climate combine to create a landscape of unparalleled beauty and diversity, where every corner of the island offers its own unique treasures to discover and explore. From the rugged cliffs of the west coast to the rolling green hills of the countryside, Ireland is a land of natural wonders waiting to be explored.

Dublin: Capital City and Cultural Hub

Dublin, the capital city of Ireland, is a vibrant and bustling metropolis that pulsates with energy and creativity. Situated on the east coast of the island, along the banks of the River Liffey, Dublin is a city of contrasts, where historic landmarks mingle with modern architecture and centuries-old traditions meet contemporary trends.

At the heart of Dublin lies its rich history and heritage, evident in its numerous historic landmarks and cultural attractions. Trinity College, founded in 1592, is one of the city's oldest and most prestigious institutions, home to the world-famous Book of Kells and the stunning Long Room library. Nearby, St. Patrick's Cathedral, founded in 1191, is a masterpiece of Gothic architecture and a symbol of Ireland's Christian heritage.

Yet, Dublin is much more than just a city of old buildings and ancient monuments. It is also a thriving cultural hub, renowned for its vibrant arts scene and dynamic nightlife. The city is home to a wealth of museums, galleries, and theaters, showcasing the best of Irish art, literature, and performance. The National Gallery of Ireland, located in the heart of the city, boasts an impressive collection of European and Irish art, including works by renowned artists such as

Caravaggio, Vermeer, and Jack B. Yeats. Dublin's literary legacy is equally impressive, with the city having produced some of the greatest writers and poets in the English language. From Jonathan Swift to Oscar Wilde to James Joyce, Dublin has long been a haven for literary talent, inspiring generations of writers with its rich history and vibrant culture. Today, the city's literary heritage is celebrated through events such as the Dublin Writers Festival and the Bloomsday Festival, which pay homage to the works of Joyce and other literary giants.

In addition to its cultural attractions, Dublin is also a thriving center of commerce and industry, with a diverse economy that spans sectors such as finance, technology, and tourism. The city is home to numerous multinational corporations, including Google, Facebook, and Twitter, which have established European headquarters in Dublin, drawn by its skilled workforce and favorable business environment.

Despite its modernity, Dublin has managed to retain its unique character and charm, with its lively street markets, traditional pubs, and friendly locals giving the city a warm and welcoming atmosphere. Whether you're exploring its historic streets, sampling its world-famous whiskey, or simply soaking up the atmosphere in one of its many parks or gardens, Dublin offers a wealth of experiences to suit every taste and interest.

Belfast: History, Conflict, and Resilience

Belfast, the capital city of Northern Ireland, is a place of deep historical significance, marked by a complex tapestry of triumphs and tribulations. Nestled on the banks of the River Lagan, Belfast has long been a center of commerce, industry, and culture, with a heritage that stretches back centuries. The city's roots can be traced to its founding as a small settlement in the early Middle Ages, which grew over time into a thriving port city, thanks to its strategic location on the Irish Sea.

In the 19th century, Belfast emerged as an industrial powerhouse, fueled by the growth of shipbuilding, linen manufacturing, and engineering. The city's shipyards, most notably the Harland and Wolff shipyard, became world-renowned for their construction of luxury liners, including the RMS Titanic. Belfast's linen mills supplied the world with fine textiles, earning the city the nickname "Linenopolis" and fueling its economic prosperity.

However, Belfast's fortunes took a darker turn in the 20th century, as sectarian tensions between the city's Protestant and Catholic communities boiled over into violence and conflict. The Troubles, a period of protracted conflict and unrest that engulfed Northern Ireland from the late 1960s to the late 1990s, cast a long shadow over Belfast, leaving scars that are still visible today. The city became a battleground, as paramilitary groups on both sides carried out bombings, shootings, and assassinations in pursuit of their respective goals.

Despite the violence and turmoil of the Troubles, Belfast has shown remarkable resilience and determination in the face of adversity. In recent decades, the city has undergone a process of regeneration and renewal, as efforts to promote peace and reconciliation have taken root. Landmark peace agreements, such as the Good Friday Agreement in 1998, have helped to bring an end to the violence and pave the way for a brighter future.

Today, Belfast is a city transformed, with its historic landmarks and cultural attractions coexisting alongside modern developments and initiatives aimed at building a more prosperous and inclusive society. The Titanic Quarter, once home to the world's most famous shipyard, has been revitalized as a vibrant waterfront district, with museums, galleries, and entertainment venues paying homage to Belfast's maritime heritage.

The city's Cathedral Quarter, named for its historic St. Anne's Cathedral, is a thriving cultural hub, with its cobbled streets lined with art galleries, theaters, and independent shops. Meanwhile, the revitalization of the Laganside area has transformed the banks of the River Lagan into a picturesque waterfront promenade, complete with parks, walkways, and outdoor recreation spaces.

Despite its troubled past, Belfast is a city with a bright future ahead, as it continues to rebuild and reimagine itself as a beacon of peace, prosperity, and resilience in the 21st century. With its rich history, vibrant culture, and resilient spirit, Belfast is a city that embodies the triumph of hope over adversity and the power of reconciliation to heal old wounds and build a better tomorrow.

Galway: Gateway to the West and Cultural Capital

Nestled on the picturesque west coast of Ireland, Galway is a vibrant and dynamic city that serves as a gateway to the rugged beauty of the Wild Atlantic Way. Known as the "City of Tribes," Galway has a rich and storied history that dates back over a thousand years, with its origins rooted in the medieval period. Founded by the Anglo-Norman de Burgo family in the 13th century, Galway quickly grew into a bustling port town, thanks to its strategic location on the shores of Galway Bay.

In the centuries that followed, Galway prospered as a center of trade and commerce, with merchants from across Europe flocking to its shores to buy and sell goods. The city's medieval streets are lined with historic landmarks and architectural treasures, including the Spanish Arch, remnants of the city's medieval fortifications, and Lynch's Castle, a fine example of Renaissance architecture.

Galway's maritime heritage is still evident today, with the bustling harbor serving as a hub for fishing boats, pleasure craft, and cargo ships. The city's waterfront promenade, known as the Long Walk, offers stunning views of Galway

Bay and is a popular spot for locals and visitors alike to stroll and soak up the atmosphere.

Yet, it is not just Galway's history that sets it apart; it is also a city of culture and creativity, with a vibrant arts scene that rivals that of any other city in Ireland. Galway is home to numerous theaters, galleries, and performance spaces, showcasing the best of Irish and international talent. The Galway International Arts Festival, held annually in July, is one of the largest and most prestigious arts festivals in Europe, attracting artists and performers from around the world.

Galway's cultural diversity is also reflected in its people, who come from all walks of life and backgrounds. The city has a reputation for being open, welcoming, and inclusive, with a strong sense of community and solidarity among its residents. The Galway Races, held each summer at the historic Ballybrit Racecourse, are a highlight of the city's social calendar, drawing thousands of spectators and horse racing enthusiasts from near and far.

In recent years, Galway has also emerged as a center of innovation and entrepreneurship, with a growing tech sector and a thriving startup scene. The city is home to numerous technology companies, research institutes, and incubators, attracted by its skilled workforce and supportive business environment. The National University of Ireland Galway (NUIG) is a leading center of research and education, with a strong emphasis on science, technology, engineering, and mathematics (STEM) disciplines.

With its rich history, vibrant culture, and dynamic economy, Galway is a city that continues to captivate and inspire all who visit. Whether you're exploring its historic streets, enjoying a traditional music session in one of its many pubs, or simply taking in the breathtaking beauty of its coastal scenery, Galway offers a truly unforgettable experience that will leave you longing to return again and again.

Cork: Rebel City and Culinary Delights

Nestled in the scenic southwest of Ireland, Cork is a city of contrasts, where rebel spirit meets culinary excellence in a delightful fusion of tradition and innovation. Known affectionately as the "Rebel City," Cork has a long and proud history of defiance and independence, dating back to its role in the Irish War of Independence and the Civil War. The city's rebellious spirit is still evident today, with its residents fiercely proud of their heritage and unafraid to challenge authority.

Yet, Cork is much more than just a city of rebels; it is also a culinary destination of international renown, with a thriving food scene that celebrates the best of Irish ingredients and flavors. The English Market, located in the heart of the city, is a bustling hub of activity, where locals and visitors alike come to sample artisanal cheeses, freshly caught seafood, and organic produce sourced from the surrounding countryside.

Cork's culinary heritage is influenced by its coastal location and rich agricultural land, with seafood and farm-fresh ingredients taking center stage on menus throughout the city. Traditional dishes such as Cork buttered eggs, spiced beef, and drisheen, a type of blood sausage, are beloved by locals and sought after by visitors eager to experience authentic Irish cuisine.

In recent years, Cork has emerged as a hub of gastronomic innovation, with a growing number of award-winning restaurants and food producers pushing the boundaries of culinary creativity. The city's chefs are renowned for their commitment to sourcing local and seasonal ingredients, resulting in dishes that are both delicious and sustainable.

Cork's food culture extends beyond the kitchen, with festivals and events celebrating everything from seafood to street food to craft beer. The Cork Oyster Festival, held annually in September, is a highlight of the city's culinary calendar, featuring oyster tastings, cooking demonstrations, and live music.

Yet, Cork's appeal goes beyond its rebellious spirit and culinary delights; it is also a city of culture and creativity, with a thriving arts scene that encompasses music, theater, and literature. The Cork Jazz Festival, held each October, is one of the largest and most prestigious jazz festivals in Europe, attracting world-class performers and enthusiasts from around the globe.

The city is also home to numerous galleries, theaters, and performance spaces, where artists and performers of all kinds come to showcase their talents. Cork's creative energy is palpable, with its streets alive with music, art, and cultural events throughout the year.

With its rich history, rebellious spirit, and culinary delights, Cork is a city that captivates and inspires all who visit. Whether you're exploring its historic streets, indulging in its world-class cuisine, or immersing yourself in its vibrant arts scene, Cork offers a truly unforgettable experience that will leave you longing to return again and again.

Limerick: A Tale of Two Rivers and Rich History

Nestled in the heart of Ireland's Shannon Region, Limerick is a city steeped in history and brimming with character. Situated at the confluence of the River Shannon and the River Abbey, Limerick's strategic location has made it a vital hub of commerce, culture, and innovation for centuries. The city's history stretches back over a thousand years, with its origins rooted in the medieval period when it was founded by the Vikings as a settlement known as "King's Island."

Throughout its long and storied history, Limerick has been shaped by its rivers, which have served as both a lifeline and a barrier to the city's development. The River Shannon, Ireland's longest river, has been a vital artery of trade and transportation, connecting Limerick to the rest of the country and beyond. The River Abbey, a tributary of the Shannon, winds its way through the heart of the city, lending Limerick its distinctive charm and character.

Limerick's rich history is evident in its many historic landmarks and architectural treasures, which tell the story of the city's past. King John's Castle, built in the 13th century by the Anglo-Norman king of England, is one of the best-preserved medieval castles in Ireland, offering visitors a glimpse into the city's medieval past. St. Mary's Cathedral, dating back to the 12th century, is another iconic landmark, with its impressive Gothic architecture and richly decorated interior.

In addition to its medieval heritage, Limerick is also known for its literary legacy, having produced some of Ireland's most celebrated writers and poets. The city is perhaps best known as the setting for the famous poem "The Ballad of Reading Gaol" by Oscar Wilde, who spent time in Limerick during his youth. More recently, Limerick has gained recognition as a UNESCO City of Literature, thanks to its vibrant literary scene and rich cultural heritage.

Despite its long history, Limerick is also a city that looks to the future, with a thriving economy and a growing reputation as a center of innovation and entrepreneurship. The University of Limerick, founded in 1972, is a leading center of research and education, with a strong emphasis on science, technology, engineering, and mathematics (STEM) disciplines. The city's Innovation District, located in the historic Georgian Quarter, is home to numerous technology companies, research institutes, and startups, attracted by Limerick's skilled workforce and supportive business environment.

With its rich history, stunning riverside setting, and vibrant cultural scene, Limerick is a city that offers something for everyone. Whether you're exploring its historic streets, soaking up the atmosphere in one of its many pubs and cafes, or simply enjoying a leisurely stroll along the riverbanks, Limerick is a city that leaves a lasting impression on all who visit.

Kilkenny: Medieval Marvels and Artisanal Crafts

Nestled in the heart of Ireland's Ancient East, Kilkenny is a city steeped in history and renowned for its medieval marvels and artisanal crafts. Founded in the 6th century by Saint Canice, Kilkenny has a rich and storied past that is evident in its well-preserved medieval buildings and charming cobbled streets.

At the center of Kilkenny's historic quarter is Kilkenny Castle, a magnificent fortress that dates back to the 12th century. Built by the Anglo-Norman Butler family, the castle is one of the most iconic landmarks in Ireland, with its imposing towers, beautifully landscaped gardens, and stunning riverside setting. Today, Kilkenny Castle is open to the public and offers guided tours that provide insight into the castle's fascinating history and the lives of its former inhabitants.

In addition to Kilkenny Castle, the city is home to numerous other medieval treasures, including St. Canice's Cathedral, a majestic Gothic cathedral that dates back to the 13th century, and Rothe House, a beautifully restored 16th-century merchant's townhouse that now serves as a museum and cultural center.

Yet, Kilkenny's appeal extends beyond its medieval heritage; it is also a city of artisans and craftspeople, with a thriving arts and crafts scene that celebrates traditional craftsmanship and creativity. The city's Design & Crafts Council of Ireland's headquarters is located in Kilkenny, showcasing the best of Irish design and craftsmanship through its exhibitions and events.

One of the highlights of Kilkenny's craft scene is the Kilkenny Design Centre, located in the historic stables of Kilkenny Castle. The center is home to a diverse array of Irish-made crafts, including pottery, textiles, jewelry, and woodwork, all created by local artisans using traditional techniques and materials.

Kilkenny is also known for its vibrant arts scene, with numerous galleries, studios, and performance spaces showcasing the work of local and international artists. The Kilkenny Arts Festival, held annually in August, is one of the oldest and most prestigious arts festivals in Ireland, featuring a diverse program of music, theater, dance, and visual arts.

In recent years, Kilkenny has emerged as a center of culinary excellence, with a growing number of award-winning restaurants, cafes, and artisanal food producers. The city's bustling food market, held every Thursday on the Parade, is a mecca for food lovers, offering a tempting array of locally sourced produce, gourmet treats, and artisanal delights.

With its rich history, vibrant arts scene, and thriving craft culture, Kilkenny is a city that offers a unique blend of old-world charm and contemporary creativity. Whether you're exploring its medieval streets, admiring its historic architecture, or sampling its delicious culinary offerings, Kilkenny is a city that captivates and delights all who visit.

Derry/Londonderry: Walls, Culture, and Reconciliation

Derry/Londonderry, often referred to simply as Derry, is a city in Northern Ireland with a rich history, vibrant culture, and a complex identity that reflects the political and social divisions of the region. The city's name reflects the dual identity it holds for its residents, with "Derry" being historically used by nationalists and "Londonderry" by unionists. At the heart of Derry's historic quarter is its iconic city walls, which date back to the 17th century and are among the best-preserved fortifications in Europe. Built between 1613 and 1618, the walls were constructed to defend the city from potential attack during the Plantation of Ulster. Today, the walls are a UNESCO World Heritage Site and a popular tourist attraction, offering panoramic views of the city and the River Foyle.

Derry's history is marked by its role in the Troubles, a period of protracted conflict and violence that engulfed Northern Ireland from the late 1960s to the late 1990s. The city was the site of several significant events during this time, including the Bloody Sunday massacre in 1972, when British soldiers opened fire on unarmed civil rights demonstrators, killing 14 people. The Troubles left a deep scar on Derry, with the city's residents bearing the brunt of the violence and suffering.

Despite the challenges of its past, Derry has made significant strides in recent years towards reconciliation and peace-building. The city's Peace Bridge, opened in 2011, is a symbol of this progress, connecting the traditionally unionist east side of the River Foyle with the nationalist west side. The bridge has become a focal point for community engagement and cross-community dialogue, fostering greater understanding and cooperation between the city's residents.

Derry's cultural scene is also thriving, with the city boasting a wealth of artistic talent and creativity. The annual Derry-Londonderry City of Culture celebrations in 2013 showcased the city's rich cultural heritage and brought international attention to its vibrant arts scene. Today, Derry is home to numerous galleries, theaters, and performance spaces, showcasing the work of local and international artists.

The city's historic Guildhall, located in the heart of the city center, is a testament to Derry's rich architectural heritage and serves as a hub for cultural events and civic gatherings. The Siege Museum, housed within the walls of the Apprentice Boys Memorial Hall, offers visitors a glimpse into Derry's turbulent past and its enduring legacy of resilience and determination.

Despite its troubled history, Derry is a city that looks to the future with optimism and hope. With its rich cultural heritage, vibrant arts scene, and commitment to reconciliation, Derry is a city that embodies the spirit of resilience and renewal, offering a beacon of hope for a brighter and more peaceful future in Northern Ireland.

Waterford: Viking Heritage and Crystal Treasures

Waterford, located on the southeast coast of Ireland, is a city steeped in history, with a rich Viking heritage and a legacy of craftsmanship that spans centuries. Founded by the Vikings in the 9th century, Waterford is Ireland's oldest city and has played a pivotal role in the country's history ever since. The Vikings established a thriving settlement on the banks of the River Suir, which became known as Vadrefjord, meaning "the haven of the ram."

The Viking influence can still be seen in Waterford today, with the city's streets and landmarks bearing testament to its Scandinavian roots. Reginald's Tower, a stone fortress dating back to the 12th century, is one of the city's most iconic landmarks and serves as a museum dedicated to Waterford's Viking past. The tower is believed to be the oldest civic building in Ireland and has stood guard over the city for over 800 years.

In addition to its Viking heritage, Waterford is also famous for its crystal craftsmanship, which dates back to the 18th century. The Waterford Crystal factory, founded in 1783, quickly gained a reputation for producing some of the finest crystal in the world, known for its clarity, brilliance, and intricate designs. Waterford Crystal became synonymous with luxury and elegance, gracing the tables of royalty, celebrities, and heads of state around the globe.

Today, visitors to Waterford can explore the city's rich heritage at the Waterford Treasures Museum, which showcases artifacts and exhibits tracing the city's history from its Viking origins to the present day. The museum's collection includes everything from Viking weapons and jewelry to medieval manuscripts and works of art.

Waterford is also known for its vibrant arts and cultural scene, with numerous galleries, theaters, and performance spaces showcasing the work of local and international artists. The city's annual Spraoi Festival, held each August, is a highlight of the cultural calendar, featuring street performances, music, dance, and theater.

Despite its ancient roots, Waterford is a city that looks to the future with optimism and ambition. The city's waterfront has been revitalized in recent years, with new developments and attractions transforming the banks of the River Suir into a vibrant and bustling hub of activity. From its Viking heritage to its crystal treasures, Waterford is a city that offers a fascinating blend of history, culture, and craftsmanship, waiting to be explored and discovered by visitors from near and far.

Wild Atlantic Way: Exploring Ireland's Spectacular West Coast

Stretching for over 1,500 miles along Ireland's rugged west coast, the Wild Atlantic Way is one of the world's most scenic coastal routes, offering breathtaking vistas, dramatic landscapes, and unforgettable experiences at every turn. This iconic driving route winds its way through nine counties, from Donegal in the north to Cork in the south, traversing some of Ireland's most spectacular scenery along the way.

The Wild Atlantic Way showcases the untamed beauty of Ireland's Atlantic coastline, with towering cliffs, secluded beaches, and windswept islands waiting to be discovered. One of the highlights of the route is the Cliffs of Moher in County Clare, rising majestically from the Atlantic Ocean to heights of over 700 feet. These sheer cliffs offer panoramic views of the ocean and the Aran Islands, making them one of Ireland's most popular tourist attractions.

Further north, in County Donegal, lies the rugged beauty of Slieve League, where towering sea cliffs plunge dramatically into the Atlantic below. These awe-inspiring cliffs are among the highest in Europe, offering spectacular views of the surrounding coastline and the wild Atlantic Ocean beyond.

The Wild Atlantic Way is also home to numerous picturesque villages and towns, each with its own unique charm and character. In County Kerry, the colorful town of Dingle is a popular stop along the route, with its quaint streets, lively pubs, and stunning coastal scenery. Nearby, the Ring of Kerry offers a scenic drive through some of Ireland's most beautiful landscapes, including rugged mountains, pristine lakes, and picturesque villages.

In County Galway, the charming village of Clifden is the gateway to the rugged beauty of Connemara, where rolling hills, sparkling lakes, and windswept moors await exploration. Further south, in County Mayo, the remote beauty of Achill Island beckons, with its rugged coastline, sandy beaches, and breathtaking sea cliffs.

Throughout the journey along the Wild Atlantic Way, visitors can immerse themselves in Ireland's rich history and heritage, with ancient ruins, medieval castles, and historic sites waiting to be explored. From the ancient stone fort of Dun Aengus on the Aran Islands to the historic fishing village of Kinsale in County Cork, the route is dotted with reminders of Ireland's past.

Whether you're driving the entire length of the route or simply exploring a small section, the Wild Atlantic Way offers an unforgettable journey through some of Ireland's most spectacular scenery. From the rugged beauty of its coastline to the warmth of its hospitality, the Wild Atlantic Way is a journey that will leave a lasting impression on all who embark upon it.

Ancient Monuments and Megalithic Sites: Mysteries of Ireland's Past

Ireland is home to a wealth of ancient monuments and megalithic sites that offer tantalizing glimpses into the mysteries of the country's past. From Neolithic burial mounds to Bronze Age stone circles, these ancient structures are a testament to the ingenuity and craftsmanship of Ireland's early inhabitants.

One of the most iconic megalithic sites in Ireland is Newgrange, located in County Meath. Built over 5,000 years ago, Newgrange is a passage tomb that predates Stonehenge and the Great Pyramids of Giza. The tomb is renowned for its intricate stone carvings and its alignment with the winter solstice, when sunlight illuminates the central chamber, marking the beginning of the new year.

Nearby, in County Louth, lies the ancient site of Knowth, which is part of the Brú na Bóinne UNESCO World Heritage Site along with Newgrange. Knowth is home to the largest collection of megalithic art in Ireland, with over 200 decorated stones featuring intricate geometric patterns and symbols.

In County Sligo, the Carrowmore Megalithic Cemetery is one of the largest and oldest cemeteries of its kind in Ireland, with over 60 Neolithic passage tombs dating back over 5,000 years. The site is surrounded by stunning views of the surrounding countryside and is thought to have been a place of ritual and ceremony for Ireland's ancient inhabitants.

Further west, on the remote island of Inishmore in County Galway, lies the ancient stone fortress of Dún Aonghasa. Perched on a cliff overlooking the Atlantic Ocean, Dún Aonghasa is one of the most impressive prehistoric forts in Europe, with its massive stone walls and dramatic setting.

In County Kerry, the Dingle Peninsula is home to a wealth of ancient sites, including the Gallarus Oratory, a perfectly preserved example of an early Christian church dating back to the 7th century. Nearby, the Dingle Stone Fort, also known as the Fahan Beehive Huts, offers a glimpse into Ireland's early Christian past, with its cluster of stone huts dating back to the 12th century.

Throughout Ireland, ancient monuments and megalithic sites continue to intrigue and inspire visitors from around the world, offering a window into the country's rich and complex history. Whether exploring the mysterious passage tombs of Newgrange and Knowth or marveling at the ancient stone forts of Dún Aonghasa and the Gallarus Oratory, these ancient sites are a testament to Ireland's enduring legacy as a land of myth, legend, and mystery.

Irish Folklore and Mythology: Legends of the Emerald Isle

Irish folklore and mythology are woven deeply into the fabric of Ireland's cultural identity, shaping the beliefs, traditions, and storytelling traditions of the Emerald Isle for centuries. From ancient Celtic legends to Christian saints and mythical creatures, Ireland's folklore is a rich tapestry of stories that reflect the country's unique heritage and imagination.

One of the most famous figures in Irish mythology is the legendary hero Cú Chulainn, whose exploits are chronicled in the epic saga known as the Ulster Cycle. Cú Chulainn, also known as the Hound of Ulster, is renowned for his bravery, strength, and prowess in battle, as well as his tragic love affair with the warrior maiden Emer.

Another iconic figure in Irish folklore is the leprechaun, a mischievous fairy creature known for his love of mischief and his pot of gold at the end of the rainbow. According to legend, leprechauns are solitary creatures who spend their days making and mending shoes and their nights causing trouble for humans who try to capture them in hopes of obtaining their treasure.

Irish folklore is also rich in tales of mythical creatures such as the banshee, a ghostly figure said to wail and keening as a warning of impending death, and the selkie, a shape-shifting seal creature that can shed its skin to become human.

The Irish countryside is dotted with ancient sites and landmarks that are steeped in legend and folklore, such as the Giant's Causeway in County Antrim, said to have been built by the giant Finn McCool as a causeway to Scotland, and the Hill of Tara in County Meath, once the seat of the High Kings of Ireland and home to the legendary Lia Fáil or Stone of Destiny.

Christianity also left its mark on Irish folklore, with saints such as St. Patrick, St. Brigid, and St. Columba becoming central figures in the country's mythology. According to legend, St. Patrick banished all the snakes from Ireland and used the three-leafed shamrock to explain the concept of the Holy Trinity to the pagan Irish.

Throughout Ireland's history, storytelling has been a central part of the culture, with tales passed down through generations by word of mouth. Today, Irish folklore continues to inspire writers, artists, and musicians, keeping alive the rich tradition of storytelling that has been a hallmark of Irish culture for centuries.

Traditional Irish Music and Dance: The Heartbeat of a Nation

Traditional Irish music and dance are deeply ingrained in the cultural fabric of Ireland, serving as a vibrant expression of the country's heritage and identity. With its roots dating back centuries, Irish music and dance have evolved over time, drawing inspiration from Celtic, Gaelic, and other cultural influences to create a unique and distinctive art form that resonates with people around the world.

At the heart of traditional Irish music is the session, a gathering of musicians who come together to play tunes, share songs, and celebrate the rich musical heritage of Ireland. Sessions can be found in pubs, homes, and community centers across the country, where musicians of all ages and abilities come together to perform and preserve the music of their ancestors.

The instruments commonly associated with traditional Irish music include the fiddle, tin whistle, flute, uilleann pipes, bodhrán, and accordion, among others. Each instrument brings its own unique sound and flavor to the music, creating a rich tapestry of melodies and rhythms that capture the essence of Irish culture.

Irish dance is another integral part of the country's cultural heritage, with its roots dating back centuries to the days of the Gaelic chieftains and warriors. Traditional Irish dance is characterized by its lively footwork, intricate patterns, and rhythmic precision, with dancers often performing in groups or solo to the accompaniment of live music. One of the most iconic forms of Irish dance is the Irish step dance, which gained international fame thanks to touring dance troupes such as Riverdance and Lord of the Dance. Step dancing is characterized by its fast-paced footwork, precise movements, and expressive choreography, with dancers often competing in regional and national competitions to showcase their skills.

In addition to step dancing, Irish ceili dancing is another popular form of traditional dance, characterized by its social and communal nature. Ceili dances are often performed in groups, with dancers joining hands and moving in intricate patterns to the rhythm of the music, creating a sense of camaraderie and connection among participants.

Throughout Ireland, traditional music and dance are celebrated at festivals, concerts, and cultural events, where locals and visitors alike come together to enjoy the music, share stories, and revel in the joy of Irish culture. From the lively reels and jigs of the dance floor to the haunting melodies of ancient ballads, traditional Irish music and dance continue to captivate and inspire audiences around the world, serving as a powerful reminder of the rich cultural heritage of the Emerald Isle.

Literary Legacy: Celebrating Ireland's Writers and Poets

Ireland's literary legacy is a testament to the country's rich cultural heritage and its enduring tradition of storytelling. From the ancient myths and legends of the Celtic bards to the contemporary works of modern writers, Irish literature has captivated readers around the world with its wit, humor, and lyrical prose.

One of the most celebrated figures in Irish literature is James Joyce, whose groundbreaking novel "Ulysses" is widely regarded as one of the greatest works of modernist literature. Set in Dublin on June 16, 1904, "Ulysses" follows the journey of its protagonist, Leopold Bloom, through the streets of Dublin, weaving together elements of myth, history, and everyday life in a kaleidoscopic narrative that revolutionized the novel form.

Another towering figure in Irish literature is W.B. Yeats, whose poetry captures the essence of Ireland's landscape, history, and folklore. Yeats was awarded the Nobel Prize in Literature in 1923 for his "inspired poetry, which in a highly artistic form gives expression to the spirit of a whole nation." His works, including "The Lake Isle of Innisfree" and "Easter 1916," continue to be cherished by readers around the world for their beauty and lyricism.

Seamus Heaney is another Nobel laureate whose poetry has left an indelible mark on Irish literature. Heaney's evocative verse explores themes of identity, memory, and the Irish landscape, earning him widespread acclaim as one of the greatest poets of the 20th century. His collections, including "Death of a Naturalist" and "North," are celebrated for their lyrical beauty and profound insight into the human condition.

Other notable Irish writers include Oscar Wilde, whose plays and essays continue to be studied and performed worldwide for their wit, satire, and social commentary; Samuel Beckett, whose existentialist plays, including "Waiting for Godot" and "Endgame," have influenced generations of playwrights and artists; and Edna O'Brien, whose novels and short stories explore themes of love, loss, and the complexities of Irish society.

In addition to its renowned writers, Ireland has a rich tradition of storytelling and oral literature, with ancient myths and legends passed down through generations by word of mouth. The stories of Cú Chulainn, Finn McCool, and the Banshee continue to captivate audiences young and old, serving as a reminder of Ireland's enduring literary heritage and its power to inspire, entertain, and provoke thought.

Gastronomic Delights: From Guinness to Gourmet Cuisine

When it comes to gastronomic delights, Ireland offers a diverse and flavorful culinary landscape that reflects the country's rich agricultural heritage, coastal bounty, and creative spirit. At the heart of Irish cuisine is a deep appreciation for fresh, locally sourced ingredients and traditional cooking techniques that have been passed down through generations.

One of Ireland's most famous culinary exports is Guinness, the iconic stout beer that has been brewed in Dublin since 1759. Known for its dark color, creamy texture, and distinctive flavor, Guinness is enjoyed by millions of people around the world and is an integral part of Ireland's cultural identity.

In addition to Guinness, Ireland is renowned for its seafood, with the country's long coastline providing an abundance of fresh fish and shellfish. From succulent oysters and plump mussels to delicate smoked salmon and hearty fish stews, Irish seafood is celebrated for its freshness and flavor, with coastal towns and fishing villages serving up some of the best seafood dishes in the country. Ireland's agricultural heritage is also reflected in its hearty and wholesome cuisine, with dishes such as Irish stew, colcannon, and boxty showcasing the country's love of potatoes, meat, and dairy products. Made with tender lamb or beef, root vegetables, and fragrant herbs, Irish stew is a comforting and nourishing dish that has been enjoyed by generations of Irish families.

Potatoes are a staple ingredient in Irish cuisine, with dishes such as colcannon and boxty featuring prominently on menus across the country. Colcannon is a traditional Irish dish made with mashed potatoes, cabbage or kale, butter, and sometimes scallions or leeks, while boxty is a type of potato pancake made with grated potatoes, flour, and baking soda.

In recent years, Ireland has experienced a culinary renaissance, with chefs and food producers embracing innovation and creativity to showcase the country's culinary heritage in new and exciting ways. From Michelin-starred restaurants serving contemporary Irish cuisine to artisanal food producers crafting gourmet cheeses, chocolates, and preserves, Ireland's food scene is thriving and diverse.

Farm-to-table dining experiences are also growing in popularity, with many restaurants and cafes sourcing ingredients directly from local farmers, fishermen, and artisanal producers. This commitment to sustainability and quality ensures that diners can enjoy the freshest and most flavorful ingredients while supporting local communities and preserving Ireland's culinary traditions for future generations to enjoy.

Whiskey, Beer, and Spirits: Ireland's Liquid Gold

In Ireland, whiskey, beer, and spirits hold a special place in the hearts of locals and visitors alike, earning the title of "liquid gold" for their rich flavors, historical significance, and cultural importance. Whiskey, spelled with an "e" in Ireland, is one of the country's most iconic exports, with a long and storied history dating back centuries. Irish whiskey is renowned for its smoothness, complexity, and distinctive flavors, which are achieved through a combination of traditional distillation methods, high-quality ingredients, and skilled craftsmanship.

The process of making Irish whiskey begins with the malted barley, which is mashed and fermented before being distilled in copper pot stills. The whiskey is then aged in oak barrels for a minimum of three years, where it develops its characteristic flavors and aromas. Irish whiskey is known for its light, fruity notes, with hints of vanilla, caramel, and spice, making it a favorite among whiskey enthusiasts around the world.

In addition to whiskey, Ireland is also famous for its beer, with Guinness being the most well-known and beloved brand. Brewed in Dublin since 1759, Guinness is a dark stout beer known for its creamy texture, rich flavor, and iconic black and white branding. The Guinness Brewery in Dublin is one of Ireland's most popular tourist attractions, offering visitors the chance to learn about the brewing process, sample different varieties of Guinness, and enjoy panoramic views of the city from the Gravity Bar.

In recent years, Ireland has seen a resurgence in craft brewing, with a growing number of small-scale breweries producing a wide range of innovative and flavorful beers. From hoppy IPAs and fruity pale ales to rich stouts and refreshing lagers, Ireland's craft beer scene is diverse and dynamic, with something to suit every palate.

In addition to whiskey and beer, Ireland is also known for its spirits, including gin, vodka, and liqueurs. Irish gin, in particular, has experienced a surge in popularity in recent years, with distilleries across the country producing a wide variety of artisanal gins infused with botanicals and flavors inspired by the Irish countryside.

Whether sipping on a smooth glass of Irish whiskey, enjoying a pint of Guinness in a cozy pub, or sampling the latest craft beer at a local brewery, Ireland's liquid gold is a cherished part of the country's cultural heritage, bringing people together to celebrate, socialize, and enjoy the finer things in life.

From Farm to Fork: Exploring Irish Food Culture

In Ireland, food culture is deeply rooted in the country's agricultural heritage, with a strong emphasis on fresh, locally sourced ingredients and traditional cooking methods. From the lush pastures of the countryside to the bustling markets of the cities, Ireland's food culture celebrates the bounty of the land and the skill of its farmers, fishermen, and producers.

At the heart of Irish food culture is a love of simple, hearty dishes made with the finest ingredients. Potatoes, for example, have long been a staple of the Irish diet, with dishes such as colcannon, champ, and boxty showcasing the versatility of this humble root vegetable. From creamy mashed potatoes to crispy potato pancakes, potatoes are a beloved and iconic part of Irish cuisine.

In addition to potatoes, Ireland's fertile soil and temperate climate support a wide variety of fruits, vegetables, and grains, including carrots, cabbage, turnips, and barley. These fresh, seasonal ingredients form the basis of many traditional Irish dishes, such as Irish stew, soda bread, and seafood chowder.

Ireland's coastline is also a rich source of seafood, with fresh fish and shellfish caught daily by local fishermen. From succulent oysters and plump mussels to tender salmon and flaky cod, Irish seafood is celebrated for its freshness and flavor, with coastal towns and fishing villages serving up some of the best seafood dishes in the country.

In recent years, Ireland has seen a culinary renaissance, with chefs and food producers embracing innovation and creativity to showcase the country's culinary heritage in new and exciting ways. From Michelin-starred restaurants serving contemporary Irish cuisine to artisanal food producers crafting gourmet cheeses, chocolates, and preserves, Ireland's food scene is thriving and diverse.

Farm-to-table dining experiences are also growing in popularity, with many restaurants and cafes sourcing ingredients directly from local farmers, fishermen, and artisanal producers. This commitment to sustainability and quality ensures that diners can enjoy the freshest and most flavorful ingredients while supporting local communities and preserving Ireland's food culture for future generations to enjoy.

The Cliffs of Moher: Majestic Beauty on the Atlantic Edge

Standing proudly on the rugged west coast of Ireland, the Cliffs of Moher are a breathtaking natural wonder that captivates visitors from around the world with their sheer beauty and dramatic scenery. Stretching for over eight miles along the Atlantic Ocean, the cliffs rise to heights of up to 702 feet at their highest point, offering panoramic views of the crashing waves below and the Aran Islands in the distance.

Formed over 300 million years ago during the Carboniferous period, the Cliffs of Moher are composed of layers of shale, sandstone, and limestone, which have been sculpted by the relentless forces of wind and waves over millennia. The result is a series of towering sea cliffs, sea stacks, and hidden caves that create a landscape of unparalleled beauty and grandeur.

The cliffs are home to a diverse array of flora and fauna, with thousands of seabirds nesting in the craggy cliffs and soaring overhead. Visitors to the cliffs can spot species such as puffins, razorbills, and guillemots, as well as kestrels, peregrine falcons, and other birds of prey. The cliffs are also an important breeding ground for seabirds, with tens of thousands of birds flocking to the cliffs each year to raise their young.

In addition to their natural beauty, the Cliffs of Moher hold a special place in Irish history and culture, with a rich heritage that spans thousands of years. The cliffs are steeped in myth and legend, with stories of giants, saints, and mythical creatures adding to their allure. According to legend, the cliffs were formed by the giant Finn McCool as a causeway to Scotland, while others believe that they were the site of battles between legendary Irish heroes.

Today, the Cliffs of Moher are one of Ireland's most popular tourist attractions, drawing over one million visitors each year to marvel at their majestic beauty and soak in the awe-inspiring views. Visitors can explore the cliffs on foot along a series of scenic walking trails, or take a boat tour to see them from the water. The cliffs are also home to a visitor center, gift shop, and café, where visitors can learn more about the history, geology, and wildlife of this iconic natural landmark.

Giant's Causeway: Nature's Masterpiece in Northern Ireland

Nestled along the rugged coastline of Northern Ireland lies one of nature's most extraordinary creations: the Giant's Causeway. This UNESCO World Heritage Site is renowned for its otherworldly landscape of hexagonal basalt columns, which stretch out across the shoreline like a giant's staircase, giving rise to its mythical name.

Formed around 50 to 60 million years ago during a period of intense volcanic activity, the Giant's Causeway is a geological marvel that continues to fascinate scientists and visitors alike. The columns were created when molten lava cooled rapidly upon contact with the cold waters of the North Atlantic, causing it to contract and crack into the distinctive polygonal shapes that we see today.

The Giant's Causeway is steeped in myth and legend, with tales of giants and warriors adding to its mystique. According to Irish legend, the causeway was built by the giant Finn McCool as a causeway to Scotland, where he could challenge his rival giant Benandonner to a duel. In reality, the causeway's formation can be attributed to the geological processes that shaped the landscape over millions of years, but the legend adds an element of magic and wonder to the site.

Today, the Giant's Causeway is one of Northern Ireland's most popular tourist attractions, drawing hundreds of thousands of visitors each year to marvel at its unique rock formations and stunning coastal scenery. Visitors can explore the site on foot along a series of well-marked walking trails, which lead through a landscape of rocky cliffs, hidden caves, and sweeping vistas of the North Atlantic Ocean.

In addition to its natural beauty, the Giant's Causeway is also home to a wealth of wildlife, with seabirds nesting in the cliffs and seals basking on the rocks below. The area surrounding the causeway is designated as a protected nature reserve, ensuring that its unique ecosystem remains preserved for future generations to enjoy.

The Giant's Causeway is not only a testament to the power of nature but also a reminder of the rich geological history of the North Atlantic region. Its striking beauty and fascinating geological features make it a must-visit destination for anyone traveling to Northern Ireland, offering a glimpse into the wonders of the natural world and the forces that have shaped our planet over millions of years.

Ring of Kerry: Scenic Splendor in the Southwest

Nestled in the picturesque southwest corner of Ireland, the Ring of Kerry is a scenic driving route that winds its way through some of the country's most breathtaking landscapes. Stretching for approximately 179 kilometers (111 miles), the Ring of Kerry encompasses rugged coastlines, rolling green hills, sparkling lakes, and charming coastal villages, offering visitors a glimpse into the natural beauty and cultural heritage of Ireland's southwest region.

The route begins and ends in the town of Killarney, a bustling hub of activity and a popular base for exploring the surrounding countryside. From Killarney, the Ring of Kerry follows a circular route around the Iveragh Peninsula, passing through towns and villages such as Kenmare, Sneem, Cahersiveen, and Glenbeigh, each with its own unique charm and character.

One of the highlights of the Ring of Kerry is its stunning coastal scenery, with dramatic cliffs, rocky headlands, and sweeping beaches stretching out along the Atlantic Ocean. Visitors can stop at viewpoints such as Ladies View and the Kerry Cliffs to admire the panoramic vistas and take in the fresh sea air.

In addition to its coastal beauty, the Ring of Kerry is also home to a wealth of natural attractions, including Killarney National Park, where visitors can explore pristine forests, tranquil lakes, and majestic mountains. The park is also home to Ireland's highest mountain, Carrauntoohil, which offers challenging hiking trails and breathtaking views from its summit.

History buffs will also find plenty to explore along the Ring of Kerry, with ancient stone forts, historic castles, and prehistoric monuments dotted throughout the landscape. One of the most famous sites is Staigue Fort, a well-preserved Iron Age fortification that dates back over 2,000 years and offers stunning views of the surrounding countryside.

Cultural enthusiasts will also appreciate the traditional music, dance, and crafts that are still practiced in the towns and villages along the Ring of Kerry. Visitors can attend local festivals, browse artisan shops, and enjoy live music sessions in cozy pubs, immersing themselves in the rich cultural heritage of the region.

Whether driving the scenic route or exploring on foot, the Ring of Kerry offers a truly unforgettable experience, with its breathtaking landscapes, rich history, and warm hospitality capturing the hearts of visitors from around the world.

Blarney Castle and Stone: Kiss the Gift of Gab

Nestled in the lush green countryside of County Cork, Blarney Castle is a historic landmark steeped in legend and lore, drawing visitors from around the world eager to kiss the famous Blarney Stone and receive the "gift of gab." The castle, built in the 15th century by the MacCarthy dynasty, stands as a symbol of Ireland's rich heritage and architectural prowess.

The Blarney Stone, located at the top of the castle's battlements, is said to bestow the gift of eloquence on those who kiss it. Legend has it that the stone was brought to Ireland from the Holy Land by Cormac MacCarthy, the builder of the castle, who believed that it held magical powers. Over the centuries, countless visitors have made the pilgrimage to Blarney Castle to kiss the stone and receive its legendary gift.

To kiss the Blarney Stone, visitors must climb to the top of the castle's battlements, lie on their backs, and lean backward over a sheer drop to reach the stone, which is set into the castle's walls. While the experience can be nerve-wracking for some, it is considered a must-do tradition for those seeking the gift of eloquence.

In addition to the Blarney Stone, the castle itself is a marvel of medieval architecture, with its imposing stone walls, turrets, and towers offering a glimpse into Ireland's turbulent past. Visitors can explore the castle's interior, which is furnished with period furniture and artifacts, and climb to the top of the battlements for panoramic views of the surrounding countryside.

Surrounding the castle is the picturesque Blarney Castle Gardens, which cover over 60 acres of landscaped grounds, woodlands, and water features. The gardens are a delight to explore, with winding pathways, colorful flower beds, and tranquil ponds providing a peaceful retreat from the hustle and bustle of modern life.

In addition to its natural beauty, the gardens are also home to a variety of rare and exotic plants, including a collection of ferns and tropical plants housed in the Fern Garden and a display of ancient Irish yew trees believed to be over 600 years old. Visitors can also wander through the Poison Garden, which is home to a variety of toxic plants and herbs with fascinating medicinal properties.

Whether seeking the gift of gab or simply exploring the historic castle and gardens, a visit to Blarney Castle is sure to be a memorable experience, offering a glimpse into Ireland's rich history, folklore, and natural beauty.

Trinity College and the Book of Kells: Treasures of Dublin

Nestled in the heart of Dublin, Trinity College stands as a bastion of Ireland's intellectual and cultural heritage, renowned for its academic excellence and historic treasures. Founded in 1592 by Queen Elizabeth I, Trinity College is Ireland's oldest university and one of its most prestigious institutions of higher learning.

One of the most famous attractions at Trinity College is the Book of Kells, a beautifully illuminated manuscript dating back to the 9th century. Created by monks in a scriptorium on the Scottish island of Iona, the Book of Kells is one of the finest examples of medieval manuscript art in the world, with its intricate illustrations and ornate calligraphy drawing visitors from far and wide.

The Book of Kells contains the four Gospels of the New Testament, written in Latin and adorned with elaborate decorations, including intricate interlace patterns, vibrant colors, and detailed illustrations of biblical scenes and figures. The craftsmanship and artistry displayed in the manuscript are truly awe-inspiring, showcasing the skill and dedication of the monks who created it.

The Book of Kells is housed in the Old Library at Trinity College, where it is displayed in a specially designed exhibition space that allows visitors to view the manuscript up close while learning about its history and significance. In addition to the Book of Kells, the Old Library is home to a wealth of other rare and valuable books and manuscripts, including early printed books, maps, and manuscripts dating back to the Middle Ages.

The Long Room, the main chamber of the Old Library, is a masterpiece of architectural design, with its soaring barrel-vaulted ceiling, rows of wooden bookshelves, and marble busts of famous writers and philosophers lining the walls. The Long Room houses over 200,000 of Trinity College's oldest and most valuable books, making it one of the most impressive library spaces in the world.

In addition to its historic treasures, Trinity College is also renowned for its academic excellence and vibrant campus life. The university offers a wide range of undergraduate and postgraduate programs across a variety of disciplines, attracting students from all over Ireland and around the globe.

Visitors to Trinity College can explore the campus on guided tours, attend lectures and events, or simply stroll through the beautiful grounds, which feature landscaped gardens, historic buildings, and modern amenities. Whether seeking knowledge, cultural enrichment, or simply a peaceful retreat from the bustle of city life, Trinity College and the Book of Kells are treasures not to be missed when visiting Dublin.

Titanic Belfast: Commemorating a Fateful Voyage

In the heart of Belfast, Northern Ireland, stands a monument to one of the most tragic maritime disasters in history: Titanic Belfast. This iconic attraction pays homage to the ill-fated RMS Titanic, which set sail from Belfast in 1912 on its maiden voyage and met its tragic end when it struck an iceberg and sank in the North Atlantic Ocean.

Titanic Belfast is located on the site of the former Harland & Wolff shipyard, where the Titanic and her sister ships, the Olympic and the Britannic, were built. The building itself is a marvel of modern architecture, designed to resemble the hull of a ship with its striking metallic façade and angular, geometric shapes.

Upon entering Titanic Belfast, visitors are transported back in time to the golden age of ocean liners, with immersive exhibits, interactive displays, and multimedia presentations bringing the story of the Titanic to life in vivid detail. The museum's nine galleries cover every aspect of the ship's construction, launch, and tragic sinking, from the design and engineering feats that went into building the Titanic to the stories of the passengers and crew who were onboard.

One of the highlights of Titanic Belfast is the Shipyard Ride, a thrilling multimedia experience that takes visitors on a virtual journey through the shipyard as it was in 1912. From the bustling workshops and slipways where the Titanic was built to the launch of the ship into the waters of the Belfast Lough, the Shipyard Ride provides a fascinating glimpse into the scale and scope of the Titanic's construction.

Another must-see attraction at Titanic Belfast is the Ocean Exploration Center, where visitors can learn about the scientific discoveries and technological advancements that have been made since the Titanic's sinking. From underwater robots and sonar mapping to deep-sea exploration and marine conservation efforts, the Ocean Exploration Center showcases the ongoing legacy of the Titanic disaster and its impact on maritime history.

In addition to its educational exhibits and interactive displays, Titanic Belfast also houses a number of artifacts and memorabilia from the Titanic and her sister ships, including personal belongings, ship fittings, and pieces of wreckage recovered from the ocean floor. These tangible reminders of the Titanic's tragic fate serve as powerful reminders of the human cost of the disaster and the enduring legacy of the ship and her passengers.

Titanic Belfast is not only a museum but also a place of remembrance and reflection, where visitors can pay their respects to the victims of the Titanic disaster and learn about the lessons that have been learned from this tragic event. By preserving the memory of the Titanic and her passengers, Titanic Belfast ensures that their stories will never be forgotten and that future generations will continue to learn from the mistakes of the past.

Kilmainham Gaol: A Journey Through Ireland's Troubled Past

Nestled on the outskirts of Dublin, Kilmainham Gaol stands as a somber reminder of Ireland's troubled past and the struggle for independence. Originally built in 1796 as a county jail, Kilmainham Gaol played a central role in Ireland's tumultuous history, serving as a place of incarceration for political prisoners and rebels throughout the 19th and early 20th centuries.

The gaol's imposing stone walls and foreboding façade are a testament to the harsh conditions endured by its inmates, many of whom were imprisoned for their involvement in the fight for Irish independence. During the 19th century, Kilmainham Gaol housed prisoners from all walks of life, including men, women, and children, who were subjected to overcrowded cells, inadequate food and sanitation, and brutal treatment at the hands of the prison authorities.

Throughout its history, Kilmainham Gaol was witness to some of the most significant events in Irish history, including the 1798 Rebellion, the Great Famine, and the Easter Rising of 1916. During the Easter Rising, the gaol became the scene of fierce fighting between Irish rebels and British forces, with many of the leaders of the rebellion being imprisoned and subsequently executed within its walls. One of the most famous inmates of Kilmainham Gaol was the Irish revolutionary leader, Robert Emmet, who was imprisoned and executed at the gaol in 1803 for his role in the failed uprising against British rule. Emmet's speech from the dock, in which he famously declared, "Let no man write my epitaph," has since become a rallying cry for Irish nationalists and a symbol of resistance against oppression. In the years following the Easter Rising, Kilmainham Gaol fell into disuse and disrepair, but its significance as a symbol of Ireland's struggle for independence was never forgotten. In 1960, the gaol was restored and reopened as a museum, dedicated to preserving the memory of those who had been imprisoned within its walls and commemorating their sacrifices in the fight for freedom.

Today, visitors to Kilmainham Gaol can take guided tours of the historic site, exploring its eerie corridors, grim prison cells, and stark exercise yards while learning about the lives and experiences of its former inmates. The museum's exhibits and displays offer a poignant and powerful insight into Ireland's troubled past, highlighting the courage, resilience, and spirit of those who fought for independence against seemingly insurmountable odds. Kilmainham Gaol stands as a testament to the enduring legacy of Ireland's struggle for freedom and the sacrifices made by those who dared to defy oppression and injustice.

St. Patrick's Cathedral: Icon of Faith and Architecture

St. Patrick's Cathedral, situated in the heart of Dublin, Ireland, stands as an enduring symbol of faith, history, and architectural splendor. Built in honor of Ireland's patron saint, St. Patrick, the cathedral is one of the country's most iconic landmarks and a testament to the enduring legacy of Christianity in Ireland.

Construction of St. Patrick's Cathedral began in 1191 on the site of an earlier church founded by St. Patrick himself in the 5th century. Over the centuries, the cathedral has undergone numerous renovations and expansions, resulting in the magnificent Gothic-style structure that we see today. Its soaring spires, intricate stonework, and majestic stained glass windows are a testament to the skill and craftsmanship of the medieval builders who constructed it.

One of the most striking features of St. Patrick's Cathedral is its interior, which is adorned with ornate carvings, elaborate altars, and beautiful religious artwork. The cathedral's nave, transepts, and choir are adorned with intricate stone carvings depicting scenes from the Bible and the lives of saints, while its stained glass windows flood the interior with colorful light, creating an atmosphere of reverence and awe.

St. Patrick's Cathedral has played a central role in Ireland's religious and cultural life for over eight centuries, serving as a place of worship, pilgrimage, and community gathering. Throughout its history, the cathedral has hosted numerous important events, including royal coronations, state funerals, and religious ceremonies, making it a focal point of national identity and pride.

One of the most famous figures associated with St. Patrick's Cathedral is Jonathan Swift, the renowned author of "Gulliver's Travels," who served as Dean of the cathedral from 1713 to 1745. Swift's legacy is commemorated with a memorial plaque and a statue within the cathedral, honoring his contributions to literature, satire, and social justice.

Today, St. Patrick's Cathedral continues to welcome visitors from around the world, offering guided tours, worship services, and cultural events throughout the year. Its serene gardens, historic monuments, and tranquil atmosphere provide a peaceful retreat from the hustle and bustle of city life, inviting visitors to reflect on the cathedral's rich history and enduring spiritual significance. As both a place of worship and a work of architectural beauty, St. Patrick's Cathedral stands as a testament to the enduring power of faith and the enduring legacy of Ireland's Christian heritage.

Irish Language and Culture: Gaeilge and Its Revival

Irish language, or Gaeilge, is an integral part of Ireland's rich cultural heritage, dating back thousands of years. It is one of the oldest written languages in Europe, with roots tracing back to the Celtic languages spoken by early inhabitants of the island. The Irish language has a unique linguistic structure, characterized by its Gaelic script and distinct phonology, making it a fascinating subject of study for linguists and language enthusiasts alike.

Throughout much of Ireland's history, the Irish language served as the primary means of communication among the native population, shaping the country's literature, music, and folklore. However, the language faced significant challenges over the centuries, including English colonization and the imposition of English as the dominant language of administration, education, and commerce.

As a result, the use of the Irish language declined steadily over time, with many native speakers being forced to switch to English in order to participate fully in society. By the early 20th century, Irish had become a minority language, spoken primarily in rural Gaeltacht areas along the western coast of Ireland, where it remained a vital part of community life and cultural identity.

In the late 19th and early 20th centuries, a cultural and linguistic revival began to take root in Ireland, fueled by a growing sense of national identity and pride. Irish language enthusiasts, known as Gaelscoil, worked tirelessly to promote the use of Irish in schools, churches, and cultural institutions, while organizations such as Conradh na Gaeilge (The Gaelic League) campaigned for the preservation and revival of the language.

The Irish Free State, established in 1922, recognized Irish as the national language and made efforts to promote its use through legislation and education initiatives. In 1937, the Irish Constitution designated Irish as the first official language of the country, alongside English, further cementing its status as a key element of Ireland's cultural identity.

In recent decades, there has been a renewed interest in the Irish language, driven by a growing awareness of the importance of preserving Ireland's linguistic heritage. The government has implemented policies to promote the use of Irish in schools, public institutions, and the media, while cultural organizations and community groups continue to celebrate the language through festivals, events, and language immersion programs.

Today, the Irish language is experiencing a resurgence, with a growing number of people across Ireland and around the world embracing Gaeilge as a means of connecting with their heritage and identity. While challenges remain, including the need for greater fluency among speakers and increased support for language revitalization efforts, the future of the Irish language looks promising, as it continues to inspire pride, passion, and a sense of belonging among those who cherish it.

Irish Hospitality: Warmth, Wit, and Welcome

When it comes to hospitality, the Irish are renowned worldwide for their warmth, wit, and genuine welcome. It's deeply ingrained in the culture, rooted in centuries-old traditions of generosity, kindness, and camaraderie.

Step into any Irish pub, and you'll immediately feel the sense of community and conviviality that permeates the air. Whether you're a local or a visitor, you'll be greeted with a smile and a hearty "Céad míle fáilte," meaning "a hundred thousand welcomes." It's not just a phrase; it's a genuine expression of hospitality that reflects the Irish spirit of inclusivity and friendliness.

Irish hospitality extends beyond the walls of the pub and into the homes of the Irish people. Inviting guests into one's home is a cherished tradition in Ireland, where visitors are treated like family and welcomed with open arms. From the moment you cross the threshold, you'll be made to feel right at home, with endless cups of tea, homemade treats, and lively conversation.

Part of what makes Irish hospitality so special is the unique blend of warmth and wit that the Irish are known for. Irish people have a natural gift for storytelling, humor, and banter, and they love nothing more than sharing a laugh and a joke with friends old and new. Whether you're swapping stories over a pint of Guinness or sharing a meal around the kitchen table, you're guaranteed to be entertained by the quick wit and lively conversation of your Irish hosts.

But perhaps the most enduring aspect of Irish hospitality is the genuine care and concern that the Irish show for their guests. From offering directions to recommending the best local attractions, Irish people go out of their way to ensure that visitors have an enjoyable and memorable experience. It's not just about providing a place to stay or a meal to eat; it's about forging connections, building relationships, and creating lasting memories.

In a world that can sometimes feel impersonal and disconnected, Irish hospitality serves as a reminder of the power of human connection and the importance of treating others with kindness, respect, and compassion. Whether you're a guest in Ireland or lucky enough to call it home, you'll find that the warmth, wit, and welcome of Irish hospitality will leave a lasting impression on your heart and soul.

Gaelic Sports: Hurling, Gaelic Football, and Rugby

When it comes to Gaelic sports, Ireland boasts a rich and vibrant tradition that spans centuries. Among the most popular and widely played Gaelic sports are hurling, Gaelic football, and rugby, each with its own unique history, rules, and cultural significance.

Hurling, often referred to as the fastest game on grass, is one of the oldest and most traditional Gaelic sports in Ireland. Dating back over 3,000 years, hurling is played with a wooden stick called a hurley and a small, hard ball called a sliotar. The objective of the game is to score points by hitting the sliotar between the opposing team's goalposts or into the net for a goal. Hurling matches are fast-paced and fiercely competitive, with players displaying incredible skill, agility, and bravery as they navigate the field amidst the chaos of flying hurleys and swinging sliotars.

Gaelic football, meanwhile, is a uniquely Irish sport that combines elements of soccer, rugby, and basketball. Played with a round ball similar to a soccer ball, Gaelic football is a fast-paced and physical game that requires a combination of speed, strength, and skill. The objective is to score points by kicking or hand-passing the ball between the opposing team's goalposts or into the net for a goal. Gaelic football matches are played on a rectangular field with 15 players on each team, and the action is non-stop from start to finish.

Rugby, while not traditionally a Gaelic sport, has gained popularity in Ireland in recent years and has become an integral part of the country's sporting culture. Rugby is a full-contact sport played with an oval-shaped ball, and the objective is to score points by carrying, passing, or kicking the ball over the opposing team's try line or between the goalposts. Rugby matches are known for their physicality, intensity, and strategic gameplay, with players engaging in scrums, lineouts, and tackles as they battle for possession and territory on the field.

All three of these Gaelic sports hold a special place in the hearts of the Irish people and play a significant role in Ireland's cultural identity. Whether it's the ancient tradition of hurling, the excitement of Gaelic football, or the camaraderie of rugby, Gaelic sports bring communities together, foster a sense of pride and belonging, and celebrate the spirit of athleticism and competition that defines Irish sport.

Pubs and Craic: Social Life in Ireland

When it comes to social life in Ireland, pubs play a central role in bringing people together and fostering a sense of community. Known for their cozy atmosphere, friendly ambiance, and lively entertainment, Irish pubs are more than just places to grab a drink; they're gathering spots where friends, neighbors, and strangers alike come to unwind, socialize, and share stories.

The word "pub" is short for "public house," and in Ireland, pubs are indeed public spaces where people of all ages and backgrounds are welcome to gather and enjoy each other's company. Whether you're a local or a visitor, stepping into an Irish pub is like stepping into a warm embrace, with the smell of Guinness in the air and the sound of laughter and conversation filling the room.

Irish pubs come in all shapes and sizes, from quaint village taverns to bustling city bars, but they all share a few common characteristics. Most Irish pubs feature a traditional wooden bar, cozy seating areas, and a wide selection of beers, whiskeys, and other libations. Many pubs also serve hearty pub grub, such as fish and chips, shepherd's pie, and Irish stew, providing the perfect accompaniment to a pint of Guinness or a glass of whiskey.

But perhaps the most important aspect of any Irish pub is the craic, a Gaelic word that roughly translates to "good times" or "fun." Craic is more than just laughter and merriment; it's a spirit of camaraderie and conviviality that infuses every interaction in an Irish pub. Whether you're striking up a conversation with the bartender, joining in a sing-along with the musicians, or sharing a joke with the locals at the bar, the craic is what makes the Irish pub experience truly special.

In addition to being social hubs, Irish pubs also serve as venues for live music, traditional Irish dancing, and other forms of entertainment. Many pubs host regular sessions where local musicians gather to play traditional Irish music, creating an atmosphere that is both lively and soulful. Others offer pub quizzes, comedy nights, or sports screenings, ensuring that there's always something happening to keep patrons entertained.

Overall, the pub is an integral part of Irish culture and society, serving as a place where friendships are forged, memories are made, and the craic is always mighty. Whether you're raising a glass with old friends or making new ones over a pint of stout, the pub is where the true spirit of Ireland comes alive, one drink and one story at a time.

Fairies, Banshees, and Otherworldly Creatures: Myths and Legends

In the rich tapestry of Irish folklore and mythology, fairies, banshees, and otherworldly creatures hold a special place, weaving tales of magic, mystery, and wonder that have captivated imaginations for centuries. These mythical beings are deeply rooted in Ireland's cultural heritage, with stories passed down through generations and woven into the fabric of everyday life.

Among the most famous of these otherworldly creatures are the fairies, or "sidhe" in Irish Gaelic, who are believed to inhabit ancient mounds, fairy forts, and hidden glens throughout the Irish countryside. Fairies are said to be beautiful and ethereal beings, possessing magical powers and an otherworldly allure that can enchant or entrap unsuspecting humans who venture too close to their domains. According to folklore, fairies are mischievous and unpredictable, capable of bestowing blessings or curses upon mortals depending on their whims.

Another iconic figure in Irish mythology is the banshee, a supernatural being associated with death and the spirit world. The banshee is said to appear as a woman dressed in white, with long flowing hair and piercing red eyes. Her mournful wail, known as the "keening," is said to foretell the death of a loved one, serving as a warning to those who hear it that death is imminent. In Irish folklore, the banshee is both feared and revered, believed to be a guardian spirit who watches over the souls of the departed and ensures they find their way to the afterlife.

In addition to fairies and banshees, Irish mythology is replete with a diverse cast of otherworldly creatures, including leprechauns, selkies, and puca. Leprechauns are mischievous tricksters who are said to hoard pots of gold at the end of rainbows, while selkies are mythical seals capable of transforming into beautiful maidens. The puca, meanwhile, is a shape-shifting creature that can take on various forms, from a horse to a rabbit to a human, depending on its mood and intentions.

These myths and legends are more than just fanciful tales; they are an integral part of Ireland's cultural identity, serving as a source of inspiration, storytelling, and spiritual connection for generations of Irish people. Whether they believe in the existence of fairies and banshees or not, the stories of these otherworldly creatures continue to captivate and enchant audiences around the world, keeping the magic of Irish mythology alive for centuries to come.

Irish Festivals and Celebrations: From St. Patrick's Day to Samhain

Irish festivals and celebrations are a vibrant tapestry woven from the threads of ancient traditions, religious observances, and cultural heritage. From the iconic St. Patrick's Day to the ancient Celtic festival of Samhain, these events provide a window into the heart and soul of Ireland, offering a glimpse of its rich history, diverse culture, and enduring spirit of celebration.

St. Patrick's Day, celebrated on March 17th, is perhaps the most famous of all Irish festivals, known around the world for its festive parades, lively music, and sea of green attire. While it originated as a religious feast day honoring St. Patrick, the patron saint of Ireland, St. Patrick's Day has evolved into a global celebration of Irish culture and heritage, marked by traditional Irish music, dancing, and of course, plenty of Guinness.

But St. Patrick's Day is just one of many festivals and celebrations that fill the Irish calendar throughout the year. In May, the city of Galway comes alive with the Galway International Arts Festival, showcasing a diverse array of music, theater, dance, and visual arts from both Irish and international artists. Meanwhile, in June, the town of Killorglin hosts the Puck Fair, one of the oldest fairs in Ireland, featuring music, dancing, and the crowning of a goat as the "King of the Puck."

In August, the Rose of Tralee International Festival takes center stage, celebrating Irish heritage and culture with parades, concerts, and the selection of the Rose of Tralee, an ambassador who represents the global Irish community. And in September, the Lisdoonvarna Matchmaking Festival brings singles from near and far together for music, dancing, and the chance to find love with the help of traditional matchmakers.

But perhaps the most ancient of all Irish festivals is Samhain, celebrated on October 31st and marking the end of the harvest season and the beginning of winter. Samhain is believed to be the origin of Halloween, with traditions such as carving jack-o'-lanterns, wearing costumes, and telling ghost stories all originating from this ancient Celtic festival. Today, Samhain is celebrated with bonfires, feasting, and rituals honoring the spirits of the ancestors.

These festivals and celebrations are more than just opportunities for revelry and merrymaking; they are expressions of Ireland's rich cultural heritage, community spirit, and zest for life. Whether you're dancing in the streets on St. Patrick's Day or lighting a bonfire on Samhain, Irish festivals and celebrations offer a glimpse into the soul of a nation that knows how to celebrate in style.

Boglands and Wildlife Reserves: Exploring Ireland's Natural Sanctuaries

When it comes to exploring Ireland's natural beauty, the boglands and wildlife reserves offer a window into the country's diverse ecosystems and rich biodiversity. Boglands, also known as peatlands, are wetland areas characterized by the accumulation of peat, a type of soil formed from decaying plant matter. These unique landscapes are home to a wide variety of plant and animal species, many of which are adapted to the acidic and waterlogged conditions found in bogs.

One of the most famous boglands in Ireland is the Bog of Allen, located in the midlands of the country. Covering an area of over 900 square kilometers, the Bog of Allen is the largest raised bog in Ireland and serves as an important habitat for rare and endangered species such as the Eurasian curlew and the hen harrier. Other notable boglands include the Connemara Bog Complex in County Galway and the blanket bogs of County Donegal.

In addition to boglands, Ireland is also home to a number of wildlife reserves and protected areas that serve as havens for native flora and fauna. The Burren National Park, located in County

Clare, is renowned for its unique limestone landscape and rich plant diversity, including rare orchids, ferns, and wildflowers. Meanwhile, the Killarney National Park, located in County Kerry, is home to Ireland's only native herd of red deer, as well as a variety of bird species, including the majestic white-tailed eagle.

Along the coast, the Saltee Islands Wildlife Reserve, located off the coast of County Wexford, provides sanctuary for seabirds such as puffins, gannets, and razorbills, while the North Bull Island Nature Reserve, located in Dublin Bay, is an important breeding ground for wading birds such as oystercatchers and redshanks.

These boglands and wildlife reserves are not only valuable for their ecological importance but also for their role in promoting biodiversity conservation and providing opportunities for outdoor recreation and nature tourism. Whether you're exploring the moss-covered landscapes of a bogland or watching seabirds soar above the waves, Ireland's natural sanctuaries offer a glimpse into the country's wild and untamed beauty.

Flora and Fauna: Discovering Ireland's Biodiversity

When it comes to the rich tapestry of flora and fauna, Ireland boasts a surprising diversity of species, despite its relatively small size. From the lush green landscapes to the rugged coastlines, the Emerald Isle is home to a wide array of plants and animals, each playing a unique role in the country's ecosystem.

Let's start with the flora. Ireland's landscapes are characterized by verdant rolling hills, dense forests, and expansive meadows, all of which provide habitats for a diverse range of plant species. The country is particularly known for its lush grasslands, which support a variety of grasses, sedges, and wildflowers such as clover, buttercups, and daisies. In the west of Ireland, the rocky terrain of the Burren is home to an astonishing array of plant life, including rare orchids, ferns, and alpine flowers that thrive in the limestone-rich soil.

Ireland's forests are predominantly made up of native species such as oak, ash, birch, and pine, providing important habitats for a variety of wildlife including birds, mammals, and insects. In recent years, efforts have been made to restore and protect Ireland's native woodlands, which have been depleted by centuries of deforestation and land clearance.

When it comes to fauna, Ireland is perhaps best known for its rich birdlife. The country is a haven for birdwatchers, with over 450 species recorded, including resident birds such as robins, blackbirds, and wrens, as well as migratory species such as swallows, sandpipers, and whooper swans. Coastal areas provide important breeding and feeding grounds for seabirds such as puffins, gannets, and kittiwakes, while inland lakes and rivers are home to waterfowl such as ducks, geese, and herons.

Ireland's mammal population includes both native and introduced species. Native mammals include red deer, badgers, foxes, and otters, while introduced species such as fallow deer, red squirrels, and hedgehogs have also established populations. Ireland's waters are home to a variety of marine mammals, including seals, dolphins, and whales, which can often be spotted along the country's rugged coastlines.

In addition to birds and mammals, Ireland is also home to a diverse range of amphibians, reptiles, and insects, including frogs, newts, lizards, butterflies, and dragonflies. These smaller creatures may not always receive the same level of attention as their larger counterparts, but they play crucial roles in the country's ecosystems, helping to pollinate plants, control pests, and maintain biodiversity.

Overall, Ireland's flora and fauna are an integral part of the country's natural heritage, providing beauty, inspiration, and ecological services that enrich the lives of both residents and visitors alike. Whether you're exploring the woodlands of Killarney, the cliffs of Moher, or the bogs of Connemara, you're sure to encounter a rich tapestry of life that reflects the diversity and resilience of Ireland's natural world.

Sustainable Tourism: Preserving Ireland's Beauty for Future Generations

In recent years, sustainable tourism has emerged as a critical priority for Ireland, as the country seeks to balance the economic benefits of tourism with the need to protect its natural and cultural heritage for future generations. With its stunning landscapes, rich history, and vibrant culture, Ireland has long been a popular destination for travelers from around the world. However, the rapid growth of tourism in recent decades has also brought challenges, including overcrowding, environmental degradation, and cultural commodification.

To address these challenges, Ireland has begun to prioritize sustainable tourism practices that minimize the negative impacts of tourism while maximizing the benefits for local communities and the environment. One key focus area is the promotion of ecotourism, which emphasizes responsible travel practices that conserve natural resources, support local economies, and promote cultural awareness and respect. Ecotourism activities in Ireland include guided nature walks, wildlife watching tours, and sustainable farming experiences that offer visitors the opportunity to learn about and engage with Ireland's natural and cultural heritage in a responsible manner.

In addition to ecotourism, Ireland is also investing in sustainable infrastructure and transportation initiatives to reduce the environmental footprint of tourism. This includes the development of eco-friendly accommodations such as eco-lodges, glamping sites, and green-certified hotels that prioritize energy efficiency, waste reduction, and local sourcing. Ireland's public transportation system has also been expanded and improved to provide visitors with sustainable transportation options, including trains, buses, and cycling routes that minimize reliance on cars and reduce carbon emissions.

Community-based tourism initiatives are another important aspect of Ireland's sustainable tourism strategy. These initiatives empower local communities to take ownership of tourism development and ensure that tourism benefits are distributed equitably among residents. Examples include community-run tours, artisan workshops, and homestay programs that offer visitors the opportunity to connect with local people, learn about traditional customs and crafts, and support small-scale enterprises that contribute to the local economy.

Furthermore, Ireland is committed to preserving its natural and cultural heritage through conservation efforts and heritage management programs. This includes the protection of national parks, wildlife reserves, and archaeological sites, as well as the promotion of sustainable practices such as responsible waste management, water conservation, and habitat restoration. By preserving Ireland's natural and cultural treasures, sustainable tourism aims to ensure that future generations can continue to enjoy and appreciate the beauty and diversity of the Emerald Isle.

Irish Art and Craftsmanship: From Pottery to Painting

Irish art and craftsmanship have a rich and storied history, dating back centuries and encompassing a wide range of mediums and styles. From pottery to painting, Ireland's artists and artisans have created works that reflect the country's cultural heritage, natural beauty, and creative spirit.

Pottery is one of Ireland's oldest and most revered crafts, with a tradition that stretches back over a thousand years. From the early days of Celtic pottery, with its intricate designs and symbolic motifs, to the modern era of studio pottery and contemporary ceramics, Irish potters have developed distinctive styles and techniques that are admired around the world. Today, pottery remains a thriving industry in Ireland, with artisans producing everything from functional tableware to decorative sculptures using traditional methods and innovative approaches.

In addition to pottery, painting has long been a popular art form in Ireland, with a rich tradition that spans centuries. From the illuminated manuscripts of the medieval monks to the landscape paintings of the Irish Impressionists, Irish artists have drawn inspiration from the country's rugged coastlines, verdant landscapes, and vibrant cities. Some of Ireland's most celebrated painters include Jack B. Yeats, Paul

Henry, and Roderic O'Conor, whose works capture the beauty and essence of the Irish countryside with remarkable skill and sensitivity.

In recent years, Ireland's art scene has experienced a renaissance, with a new generation of artists and craftsmen embracing traditional techniques while also pushing the boundaries of contemporary art. From vibrant street murals to experimental installations, Irish artists are exploring themes of identity, history, and social change, creating works that challenge and inspire viewers.

Craftsmanship is also alive and well in Ireland, with artisans working in a variety of disciplines such as woodworking, metalworking, and textiles. Traditional crafts such as knitting, lace making, and basket weaving continue to thrive, with artisans preserving and passing down centuries-old techniques to future generations. Meanwhile, contemporary craftsmen are putting a modern spin on traditional crafts, creating innovative and stylish products that reflect Ireland's rich cultural heritage.

Overall, Irish art and craftsmanship are integral parts of the country's cultural identity, reflecting its history, landscape, and people. From the skilled hands of the potter to the visionary eye of the painter, Ireland's artists and artisans continue to create works of beauty and significance that captivate and inspire audiences both at home and abroad.

Irish Fashion and Design: Contemporary Style with Celtic Flair

Irish fashion and design have undergone a remarkable evolution in recent years, blending contemporary style with traditional Celtic influences to create a unique and vibrant aesthetic that resonates both at home and on the international stage. From haute couture to streetwear, Irish designers are making waves with their innovative designs, quality craftsmanship, and commitment to sustainability and ethical production practices.

One of the defining characteristics of Irish fashion is its emphasis on craftsmanship and quality materials. Many Irish designers draw inspiration from the country's rich textile heritage, incorporating traditional Irish fabrics such as tweed, linen, and wool into their collections. These materials not only lend a sense of authenticity to Irish fashion but also reflect the country's natural beauty and rural heritage.

In addition to traditional textiles, Irish fashion designers are also known for their innovative use of modern materials and techniques. From cutting-edge sustainable fabrics to 3D printing technology, Irish designers are constantly pushing the boundaries of what is possible in fashion, creating garments that are both stylish and environmentally conscious.

Celtic symbolism and motifs also play a prominent role in Irish fashion and design, with many designers drawing inspiration from ancient Celtic art and mythology. From intricate knotwork patterns to symbolic imagery such as the Claddagh ring, these elements add a distinctive flair to Irish fashion, infusing it with a sense of history and heritage.

Irish fashion designers are not only known for their creativity and craftsmanship but also for their commitment to sustainability and ethical production practices. Many designers prioritize locally sourced materials and small-scale production methods, ensuring that their garments are both eco-friendly and socially responsible. Additionally, initiatives such as the Sustainable Fashion Dublin collective are working to promote sustainability and ethical practices within the Irish fashion industry, raising awareness and inspiring positive change.

In recent years, Irish fashion has gained recognition on the global stage, with Irish designers showcasing their work at prestigious events such as London Fashion Week and Paris

Fashion Week. From established names such as Simone Rocha and JW Anderson to up-and-coming designers like Richard Malone and Aoife McNamara, Irish fashion talent is making its mark on the international fashion scene, garnering praise for its creativity, craftsmanship, and unique perspective.

Overall, Irish fashion and design are thriving, blending contemporary style with Celtic flair to create a distinctively Irish aesthetic that celebrates the country's heritage and creativity. Whether it's a handcrafted Aran sweater, a bespoke tailored suit, or a cutting-edge streetwear ensemble, Irish fashion offers something for everyone, embodying the spirit of innovation, craftsmanship, and individuality that defines the Emerald Isle.

Planning Your Trip: Practical Tips and Insider Insights

Planning your trip to Ireland is an exciting endeavor, filled with anticipation for the adventure that awaits. Whether you're a first-time visitor or a seasoned traveler, there are a few practical tips and insider insights that can help ensure your journey is smooth, memorable, and enjoyable.

First and foremost, it's essential to do your research before you go. Ireland is a diverse and dynamic country, with a wealth of attractions, activities, and experiences to offer. Take the time to familiarize yourself with the various regions of the country, from the bustling cities of Dublin and Galway to the scenic countryside of County Kerry and the rugged coastline of County Donegal. Consider what interests you most – whether it's history, culture, outdoor adventure, or culinary delights – and tailor your itinerary accordingly.

When it comes to accommodations, Ireland offers a wide range of options to suit every budget and preference. From luxurious five-star hotels to cozy bed and breakfasts, self-catering cottages, and boutique guesthouses, there's no shortage of places to stay. Keep in mind that accommodations in popular tourist destinations can book up quickly, especially during peak season, so it's a good idea to book your accommodations well in advance to avoid disappointment.

Transportation is another important consideration when planning your trip to Ireland. While the country is relatively small compared to other European destinations, it's worth noting that driving distances can be deceiving due to narrow roads and scenic detours. If you plan to explore beyond the major cities, renting a car can offer the flexibility and freedom to travel at your own pace and discover hidden gems off the beaten path. However, if you prefer not to drive, Ireland also has an extensive public transportation network, including trains, buses, and ferries, that can take you to most major destinations.

When packing for your trip to Ireland, it's essential to be prepared for the country's famously unpredictable weather. The Emerald Isle is known for its rain, so be sure to pack waterproof clothing, including a sturdy raincoat and waterproof boots. Layering is key, as weather conditions can change quickly, especially in coastal areas. Don't forget to pack a few warm layers, including sweaters, scarves, and hats, even if you're visiting in the summer months.

Finally, don't be afraid to venture off the beaten path and explore some of Ireland's lesser-known attractions and hidden gems. While popular tourist destinations such as the Cliffs of Moher and the Ring of Kerry are undoubtedly stunning, Ireland is also home to countless off-the-beaten-path treasures waiting to be discovered. Whether it's a secluded beach, a charming village, or a historic castle off the tourist trail, these hidden gems can provide a unique and authentic glimpse into Ireland's rich cultural heritage and natural beauty.

Overall, planning your trip to Ireland is an exciting opportunity to explore a country rich in history, culture, and natural beauty. By doing your research, booking accommodations in advance, and being prepared for the unpredictable weather, you can ensure that your journey to the Emerald Isle is a memorable and enjoyable experience from start to finish.

Epilogue

As we come to the end of our journey through the captivating landscapes, rich history, and vibrant culture of Ireland, it's worth reflecting on the experiences we've shared and the memories we've made along the way. From the ancient monuments of Newgrange to the bustling streets of Dublin, from the rugged cliffs of Moher to the serene beauty of the Ring of Kerry, Ireland has left an indelible mark on our hearts and minds.

Throughout this book, we've explored the fascinating history of Ireland, from its ancient Celtic roots to its modern-day emergence as a vibrant and dynamic nation. We've delved into the struggles and triumphs of its people, from the Viking invasions and Norman conquests to the more recent struggles for independence and peace. We've marveled at the country's natural beauty, from its lush green landscapes to its dramatic coastlines and rugged mountains.

We've also discovered the rich tapestry of Irish culture, from its traditional music and dance to its literary legacy and culinary delights. We've learned about the warmth and hospitality of the Irish people, their resilience in the face of adversity, and their enduring spirit of creativity and innovation.

As we bid farewell to Ireland, let us carry with us the memories of the sights we've seen, the sounds we've heard, and the tastes we've savored. Let us remember the stories we've heard and the friendships we've forged along the way. And let us take with us the spirit of Ireland – its beauty, its history, and its people – as we continue on our own journeys, wherever they may lead.

In the end, Ireland is more than just a place on a map – it's a state of mind, a feeling of connection to something greater than ourselves. It's a reminder of the power of nature, the resilience of the human spirit, and the importance of cherishing the moments we have together. So as we say goodbye to Ireland, let us carry its spirit with us always, knowing that it will forever hold a special place in our hearts.

Made in the USA
Columbia, SC
16 July 2025

60812639R00063